Selected Poems

By Terence Mark Winstead

ISBN-13: 978-1727803280

ISBN-10: 1727803280

Dedication

This book is dedicated to my late mother, Jean D. Winstead. She was always the first one I ran to with my latest poem. I miss her and love her profoundly.

Acknowledgements

Among the coldness, cruelty and indifference of the greater world, I cherish H.N. She is only warmth, spirit, and light. She continues to bring out my best.

The Tulip

A tulip has dreams of being

A rose to some in the seeming

Looking over tall grass seeing

A rose is a tulip in the dreaming

The way the thorny curse says a rose

The tulip's aquiline stem responds

Unlike the petty midwife's bickering root

The tulip's long waist lilting flute

Carrying the tulip's ambitious yearnings

Not dry, not arid, not falsely said

Not planting poison in the rose's bed

Not coveting her endless silky folds

But modeling where nature, beauty molds

The rose, whose inheritance it is

To inspire sweet verse as buried deep

As imbedded headstones of the tiara

Is but the tulip whispering in its sleep.

To innocence I once knew

Reach back and grope in dark

With avid eyes employ worn prints

To spur a smile with brights

And grays likewise to find the mood

To fit the hue and frames of mind

Know firm footings climb the slide

And lose all jade on one wild ride

Through sound and sight

A pattern makes plain the most bizarre of tale

And take a pal and make him young

A plus to all, a pain to none

And mother's sweep would cure all ills

And magic carpets hid all evils

And I had eyelids.

Passionate

When one exclusive portrait paints my dreams

Makes light or shade with just a single brush

I live, but for the moments next

I die, but I may live again

Depending on the stroke of fate

This woman stands subject to all my thoughts

She poses, still in ambiguity

She poses, painted unaware

She paints, the posies in her hand

Deflowered one by one by one

How patient she sits, stands my invasion

While my mind doctors her every aspect

Who knows? Perhaps she smiles for me

Who knows, but doesn't know the truth

Ignorant that I know it all

With love permeating my every pore

And passion flooding me with flowing lines

I dab, and reconcile the flame

I hide, affecting modest hues

Where everything is blazing red

My urgent tongue cannot forebear the news

So furious the rash of sentiment

It breaks, and punctuates the point

It needs, and then accenting thus

My love is worthy of my love.

The Sidewalk and the Sand

I close my eyes once more

And think my thoughtful wish

Of holding you at night

Your breath the same as mine

Of walking through your dream

And reaching to you while

We contemplate the sea

Your thought the same as mine

The sidewalk and the sand

Holding hands as we

And they are like we too

Not always two agree

But walking through a dream

The sidewalk and the sand

Do contemplate the sea

And hold each other's hand.

Interlude

Breaking in on two lovers in minuet

Popping the shades on a sunlight symphony

Bounding down three flights of stair

Taking the fourth in a heist of ecstasy

A pinch on the wrist before a pinch

Of regret is tossed over the shoulder

Between two full and luscious heads snarling in repartee

Soft satin sheen from here to eternity

Of Morgans, coy in waiting to be mounted

The first bead of sweat breaking the surface

From the most active volcano in the deepest

Widest coldest Arctic ocean of human flesh

A woman's mind racing, running down

Overtaking Pegasus of the ultimate phallus

A man's mind cleared like a ruptured hourglass

A gigantic mountainous wave of pleasure

Exploding from both toward each other

In resolution of all the days doings, trite and trivial

A roar from magnificent Eros of the golden mane

 Becomes a whisper soft suggestion of mutual satisfaction

Celibacy is the name of the child yanked

In fury from the keyhole of Heaven's door.

Palms

On the reverse of your palm is a plan for living

Know it well

Memorize the hairs that grow, promise

Fall away without notice

Think yourself a hot air balloon

With textbooks for ballast

The heart fires the head

Whenever it turns liability

Ambitions are dismissed

When directions defy directives

Brand new pencils can be sharpened away

Even you will let you down sometimes

But ever so gently.

The Seesaw

A seesaw is a way to fly

A way to teach the kids to help

Each other in their wish to ride

A dolphin leaping from the sea

And it's the same for you and I

A kind of trampoline it is

A way to send you higher than

Your feelings can lift you alone

So you are down and I am up

But see how fast the teeter tots

Then you are up and I am down

And it's a game of endless tag

And would it were my panting heart

Could slide you to my happy side

And catch you laughing in my arms

As laughing now I write for you

A seesaw is a ferris wheel

I ask you now to ride with me

And I will kiss you secretly

When we are floating on the air.

Another Moment Lived

Solemn, somber form spread eagle

Inviting justice, peace, tranquility

Instead pain, disillusionment arrive

Turn out in droves

Invite the white, plain clothes sense of sensibility

To preside over meal

No response elicited, but much rotation

And blindingly slow revolution, orbiting innocence

The guests titter, restlessly, stroke the atmosphere

While nature tends to its chores and time sleeps

Send me and mine to sheltered cloak

While brilliant bodies bathed in flame swiftly pass

Overwhelming passions feast and become memory

Chance to go?

No, stay and watch the season display its wares

Comes March to deceive

Allow all, no bitterness

Nestle myself in the arms

And peer lovingly into the face of the clock.

No woman takes me, seriously or not

My love wears a beanie, propeller and all

And every romance pulls on pajamas

My coolest, suavest approach dangles candy cigarettes

The Casanova in me carries change, but no cold hard cash

Even Casa isn't who he says he is

Leading me down the primrose littered personal ad path

And I guarantee everyone will crimp their necks

Looking sideways at any fool wearing flip flops

Anyplace but down Avenue Sandy View

Otherwise known as the beach.

Snicker at the time immemorial

First hazy rays debuting on a stark horizon

Reigning superior against the back of leisure

And minds are made up

Seconds cringe, cowards to a conflict

Are whole hewn, are slaughtered in mass

And minds are made up

Third degree burns commingle convincingly

For the future, for the greater good of man

But minds are made up

Fourthly breaks the trinity

Allowing froth, winnowed

The deceased fly to the firmament or away

Their minds are made up

Fifteen past the hour of reconciliation

And all walk through the valley of shadow

To a man.

Tying the Knot

This woman I loved married a man

Who couldn't tie his shoe laces

Didn't particularly care for her

Was the man of her dreams

When he climbed a ladder

She held it steady

Wondering in multitudinous ways

How he would one day return the favor

In fall, I helped her clean her gutters

She held the ladder while I swept the leaves

She wondered if she owed me

I smiled silently, confident I could tie both of our shoe laces

She asked how much longer it would take

I told her not long, any day now.

I never cry

"I made you cry!"

In mockery

My girlfriend said

At least I heard

"I made you cry!"

I never did

She said it, but

I must deny

So, what would make

My girlfriend say

"I made you cry!"

I never do

Oh, honey, well

The joke's on you

My eye is dry

I never cry!

Maybe

If lives are a day

We've lived so long

We've talked as if

Ours never could end

We've talked through nights

Until morning's come

We've walked through walls

Of absurdity

We've wandered, waded

Into the dark

We've come out, laughing

Into the light

This may be the morning

This may be the night

Maybe mid afternoon

On a perfect day.

Love is a raging fiction

Raging fiction

Now recruiting new members

This means you!

Stay forever young in an epic story about perfect love

Raging fiction

Sign up now

Be the first one on your block

Are you hurting?

Looking for answers?

Come to us

We'll talk.

A little birdy told me

We gave the park bench purpose

Your legs kicked

A cheery, flush faced young girl scout

Sold us a box of mint chocolate cookies

Just myself and my bluebird

On a park bench perch, chirping away

The girl scout was furtively watching

Naïve but knowing in the breaking July heat

She glimpsed her future in disappointing men

In the warm, melted chocolate oozing out the edges

In the hot, sticky tears oozing out the eyelids

In her blunt rejection oozing out much too easily

For me to reconcile

Her hands wringing, us beating a retreat

She had every reason to call out

She wanted to, but decided not.

Taller than me

Trees, bend a while

I need the comfort of knowing

I'm not alone in a world of iron and stone

And stony faces and shirts that need ironing

Canoeing in a helix

Paddling like the living

Ending with the dying

Pulling me down into the murky depths

When I want the sky you can dip to me

Collect me in your loftiest branches

Tease me with your leafy ticklers

Can let me laugh

And share it with the next hungry, passing giraffe.

Hanging in

Loyalty is coming back when the going is better

Going a good deed better

Forgetting the extra give

Covering the bettor at his table

Settling for no answer, expecting

On a pregnant matter to a lover the question put

Knowing when to play the macaw

Scrubbing away the word "betray"

Commonly packing most people's otherwise pure intentions

For a friend or lover or another

It's cutting a coat from a door jam

Wrangling a shoe from a train track

Unsticking a chum from predicament

You're only too happy to find yourself in.

I heard you laugh

I heard you laugh

As we sat for a play

There was a man, a woman

And he delivered a line

It was to the effect that

He loved her and would

Always tell her in this way

Dramatically and with heart

He laughed and as he said it

She laughed to make him happy

Which you found so funny

That you started laughing

I was so happy myself

I looked from him to her

To you, and then surprisingly

I started laughing too.

Two heads

I saw a woman with two heads

Both silky blond and turned away

How many people did I see?

How many could have looked at me?

Oh how she cooed and made a sound

Just like a mother with her child

And how she cooed and answered back

But like a newborn only can

And this poor woman was so far

That I would simply have to guess

How this cursed woman had two heads

But she could still seem quite content?

And then before I sadly went

This woman turned herself to me

I saw her baby that did coo

It made me wish for two heads too.

Around a fire

A group of friends

Sit around a fire

One is too close

And does perspire

One is too small

And does not count

Astronomers constantly

Debate the amount

Of friends around the fire

One wears a ring

And seems to be wed

His neighbor in size

Is slightly ahead

Circling the fire on

An infinite night

A group of friends

Make a galactic sight

Around a blazing fire.

The Salmon

I went to a river

And saw salmon struggle

To get to the source of

Whatever impelled them

It made me quite anxious

To see something foolish

In creatures of impulse

Not stopping to think

I wanted to ask them

What is it that has you

So frenzied and driving

And jostling the others?

But dizzy with questions

I got in my car and

I fought with the traffic

Until I was home.

Love is a sleeping cat

An old man sat

Rocking on a porch

With an old woman

And a cat between them

The couple had been

Sitting for years

They wouldn't get up

Because of the cat

And how peculiar

The way they sat

Living their lives

And the sleeping cat

Was never asleep

And watched them both

Through one eye slit

Contentedly.

I have seen flowers

I have seen flowers grow

In patches of ice and

Seen a rainbow through

The thickest fog

I have seen rain fall

From a cloudless sky

I've been struck by

The lightning of an idea

Been caught in the storm

Of a pleasant day and

Seen the moon steal

The role of the sun

I have seen flowers grow

In patches of ice and

I will see a woman's love

Before I am gone.

Two lights

There is a house

With two lights on

They never go out

No matter what happens

If people are there

Or no one's home

It makes no difference

The lights will stay

Those same two lights

Are lighting the house

And keeping the darkness

From entering in

They keep each other

From being lonely

When the house is full

Or completely empty

It makes no difference

To those two lights

Which are always on

And there for each other

If no one is there

There's one for the other

As those two lights

Will never go out.

Funny how we trade

A child buys shoes

To grow into, while

His mother tries to

Shrink into her jeans

A man takes time out

To tailor his suit

Two words that mean

The same as each other

Funny how we trade

The one for the other

While the grass fades

Each side to a brown

See the business people

Going to town, only

So they can buy the life

That waits in the country.

The story of a horse

The story of a horse

Who climbed a tree

Never made the papers

Though it was unusual

In the time it was done

He was the only one

Who felt the inclination

To try something new

Knowing no horse before

Had seen what he would

He knew the experience

Would be good for horses

Though he made it, then

Fell and broke his neck

From the edge of his eye

He saw a rocket take off

It looked like a horse

In a cluster of wood

Roaring upward, aflame

Till it reached the branches.

I ain't a cat

I ain't a cat

I ain't so cool

Cause cats don't cry

But this one do

You ever seen

A cat did cry?

A cat in pain'll

Make a noise

Like nothing else

But never cry

And all I know's

I ain't no cat

Another thing

A cat won't do

Is tell you that

He ain't no cat.

I am a bird

I am a bird

Upon the lea

Wanting to feed

I pecked a seed

It wasn't a seed

I let it fall

I pecked again

It wasn't a seed

I pecked a third

And nothing, it

Was not a seed

I'm not a bird

There is no seed

There is no lea

This poem is

Not about a seed.

The farmer, the sailor

The sailor stood

Behind the bow

And reckoned

His acres of ocean

The farmer stood

Behind the plow

And reckoned

His waves of grain

They both upon

The sky did gaze

And wished for

Cooperation

The sailor stood

Behind the plow

The farmer stood

Behind the bow.

There is a night

If there is a morning

There is a night

A rich man fears

His money will go

A desperate man

His lover too

If there is a rising

There is a fall

A winner knows

His loss awaits

A young man feels

His coming age

The blinded saw

The end of sight

If there is a morning

There is a night.

The little black eyed rabbit

A little black eyed rabbit

Sat and studied the world

His body started shaking

As he took it all in

A horror and an ugliness

Were all he could see

His little black eye staring

Most disconsolately

His body shaking harder

As it grew in his eye

This overwhelming evil

That could not be ignored

The little black eyed rabbit

Is inside you and me

And trembling at the sight

Of things that no one should see.

The Bus

I'll wait and see

But will it come?

The day is short

But getting on

There is a bus

But only one

I'll wait and see

But will it come?

I want the bus

Just to myself

I hope the other's

Getting off, and

When it stops here

Will it go?

Or find another

On its way?

The bus will be

Here before long

I've got one chance

For getting on

I'll wait and see

But will it come?

There is a bus

But only one.

I am to be stung

Climbing up the tree

Reaching for the comb

Like paws into a jar

It is not long, it is not far

Close it is, but closer now

And I am nearly there

So sweet and dripping, love

But much as now I strive

I cannot be too nonchalant

There is a hidden hive

And I am to be stung

This tree that I have clung

Is love and nothing but

The bees are coming on

And I am loving honied you

But I am to be stung

Then what's the worth of loving you?

You were not long, and then you flew

Stinging me, I drew from you

You came for me, then spun

You went away, I waved goodbye

To love, I have so clung

I surely would be stung

For I am just a bear

Who'd breathe your honied air

I was so nearly there

But I am to be stung.

A boat is a car is a boat

I'm in a boat

But I'm in a car

The river goes

The highway goes

The gray waters

The blue pavement

The rapids and

The fast lane

The paddle

The pedal

The on ramp

The tributary

The splash

The crash

The drowning

The drowning

Do you know you have a tail?

Do you know you have a tail?

A story that goes on behind you?

It follows you wherever you go

And comes around to confront you

It comes in a dream sometimes

And speaks in images and words

Sometimes it's buried in conversation

And comes around as a memory

Our tails are really our history

And grow the extent of our lives

If animals are identified by theirs

Why should we be any different?

I'm eager to know who you are

And why I am wanting to curl

So protective around you at night

As if I am your tail.

The Dandelion

A dandelion is

A flower, a weed

A way of

Seeing the world

A youthful hand

Will pull it up

A graying mind

Will cut it down

Hardy but delicate

It is the world

Roaring sunshine

Gloomy silence

A kiss on the cheek

To a little girl

Powerful medicine

To an old woman

And like both in

Stages of life

Yellow haired

But turning gray.

The Heaviest Word

This is the tale

Of the heaviest word

Some say it is

Impossible to lift

Many have tried

To raise it from

The lonely place

It weighs the ground

Legend has, if

Moved an inch

To one's surprise

It floats away

Too heavy to lift

Too light to stay

"Love" remains

The heaviest word.

A little boy and girl

The hottest day in summer

On the streets of a city

A little boy and girl

Race around together laughing

Stripped to shorts and tanks

Shoeless and careless

The boy in his madness

Chasing after the girl

Running through a theatre

A church, across a beach

Splashing through several

Wine soaked conversations

The calendar pages fly

Float, blanket the streets

And the little boy cries out

"I love you!" to the girl.

The giant of conventional thinking

Shatter the window

And make it explicit

Fracture convention

Take reality with it

We believe so big

And know so little

Just topple the giant

And watch him struggle

Life is a house

We have to break in

Inside is the giant

Committing a sin

The house, the giant

The lie, the sin

Just shatter the window

We have to break in!

The dragon and the unicorn

A dragon, a unicorn

Met in a cell

Unhappy prisoners

Of a fairy tale

They said, "We can talk

Us out of jail."

The conversation

Went something like this,

"If you're not real

Then neither am I

But I know that I am

So you must be too."

There's was a logic

That allowed them to flee

No longer held captive

To a fantasy.

The furious peace

The day of the furious peace

Not a thing was broken

Not the skin of a man

Not the heart of a woman

The hope of a child

Remained intact

A policeman

Didn't overreact

The bullets slept

Soundly in their casings

A perceived slight

Ended in a hug

Everyone, everywhere

Caught the peaceful bug

On that remarkable day

Of the furious peace.

The lady came down

The lady came down

A sparkling staircase

Slow descending, floating

To the landing

Gracefulness and light

She trails, the breath

Of everyone taken away

The room she enters

Starts to say....

But oohs and ahhs

Replace all words, and

Me in an awestruck

Silence of my own

Standing, expecting

My nervous heart thumping

On that glorious day

The lady came down.

The snow on the mountain

Philosophy can only go so high

and then it can't progress,

like climbers in a mountain snow

Who think they know, but aren't equipped.

They set out climbing anyway,

but never make it to the top.

Just look at how the peaceful climbers

Sun themselves in snowy sand.

How many thinkers met their end?

Lie frozen stiff just short of God.

With Cards

So many things

To do with cards

Just like with a

Relationship

Can be devoted

Or instead, can

Fold it in

And go astray

Can be someone

Who keeps their word

Or plays around

And dates a third

So many things

That one can do

When in a game

Of cards for two

Can build a house

Or merely play

Can make a royal

King and queen

Or be the Jack

Philandering

So many things

To do with cards

Can play a trick

Or be amazing

Gamble all your chips away

Can be committed

Or just play

So many things

To do with cards.

The Bluffs

Won't you show me, won't you please?

What is there beyond the bluffs?

The sun came down so many times

its shadows casting purple blues

I cannot see, I wish to be

much taller than I'm presently

I need to know, so will you tell?

Oh, what is there beyond the bluffs?

Are mountains looming larger

or are smaller dunes beyond the glen?

What is further then?

Won't you show me, won't you please?

What is there beyond the bluffs?

A monster lay awake

A monster hid

Under the sheets

He lay in bed

But couldn't sleep

Was frightened of

A little boy

Under his bed

And threatening

The monster tried

In vain, to tell

Himself the boy

Could not be real

With nightmares

Entering his head

A monster lay

Awake in bed.

The broken law

A man did err

And broke the law

He thought, "But then

The law will heal!"

He saw it as

A broken bone

If given time

Would be like new

Then in his cell

He found it true

The doctor said

"It will repair.

I think we'll have

To keep you here

Until the bone

Is whole again."

The fussy baby

Fussy baby, why do you fuss?

What is there that has to be

Invisible to all of us

And will not let a baby sleep?

How I wish that you could say

Just what it is that makes you cry

Fussy baby, knowing I

Can never, ever really know.

Into the trees

Oh, beautiful creature

So given to ease

You stood at the wood

And looked at the trees

I moved so close

You looked at the wood

My face was pleading

You looked at the wood

In looking again

You'd moved away

You'd done as you would

At the end of the day

I tried, but couldn't

Convince you to stay

Oh beautiful creature

So moving with ease

You left me and

Went to the trees.

I want to make the day

A pot is made of clay

A pot can hold the earth

The earth is made of clay

And clay is earthen too

A pot is filled with soil

That's taken from the earth

I left it on the sill

In hopes you're passing by

Are you the lovely rose

That searches for a home?

Then step into my soil

I put it there myself

The sun is sunny rays

That hold the sun entire

A sunny blazing fire

Scorching through the rays

The sun is burning up

And cooling as it heats

To whom the sunshine meets

It warms and raises up

Are you the lovely rose

That shivers for the sun?

Then step into my rays

I ordered them myself

The water is of drops

And drops the water, too

When cloudy sponges sop

Then find the weight's too much

Like flowers in a drought

That find the wait's too long

And clouds above don't hear

The pleading of their tongues

Are you the lovely rose

That's pleading of the sky?

I'll let a shower fly

And sprinkle it myself

Then God is in my hands

As I was once in God's

I press my hands in prayer

And I am pressing his

Oh, wisest God, so wise

Help me make the day

And shape it of a clay

That sticks and sticks, oh please.

The caution of the ocean

"Caution, the Ocean"

Wading with you

The waters grow deeper

But maybe it's us

Growing less able

But we can still see

Tip of our toes now

With heads tilted back

Forward to land, look

Backward to shore

Gasping and splashing

We struggle sometimes

Our feet can touch bottom

So we are still safe

Yet still I am going

Out further with you

And it isn't funny

We're starting to drown!

Oh, what've I done

By ignoring the signs?

"Caution, the Ocean"

Oh, what did it mean?

All I am doing

Is taking you out

Further and further

And further we go

Deeper and deeper

But isn't that right?

And I'm only doing

What all of us do

When meeting that someone

Who makes us see love

Go deeper and deeper

Wade into the night

The welcoming waters

Invited us in

And all of the signs

Meant nothing to me

But now we are drowning

I'm able to see

That "Caution, the Ocean"

Was never more clear

And it is just sadness

That we didn't heed

The warning, so painted

On all of the signs

Is rotting and fading

And being ignored.

In a park on a Sunday

An old man watched a young couple

In a park on a Sunday morning

He knew neither, didn't want to scare

Them away in their romantic puberty

The boy went, gathered a flower

Shyly gave it to the blooming girl

The girl, coy, gave the boy a kiss

You had to be quick to catch it

The old man lifted up his hand

Touched a finger to his drying lips

The girl first, then the boy behind

Slowly stationed themselves by a tree

They hugged and held the hug as long

As their youthful bodies could take

The old man felt a tremble pass

Through his elderly, graying frame

The two, now smiling, looking down

Turned and slowly walked away

Holding hands, they were quiet

And the sun was coming up

The old man had to wipe the tears

Clouding more, his aging, cloudy eyes

A moment, then he rose to leave

Just as the sun began to set.

I made a woman leave

I made a woman leave

But I did not intend

To give her a reason

To say goodbye to me

In my feelings for her

I offered her my heart

But she handed it back

A present unopened

In our hunger for love

We act as if a wolf

Had brought us a meal

For we are cold and starved

But not trusting the wolf

We turn the meal away

Since after all is said

It was brought by a wolf!

Or maybe like a bird

Who is offered a seed

We quickly fly away

Never trusting the hand

We are like this with love

And we go away empty

Leaving tracks in the snow

Leaving traces in the sky.

The boomerang

If you throw a boomerang

It always comes back

It's the principle in action

Of reciprocity

It requires that a good

Be traded for a good

It's an equal application

In regard to evil

So if I pat you

You will pat me back

If I pat too hard

I will lose a friend

For good or for ill

I will launch my acts

Then they fly the world

And doubling back

I pray that when

They find my hand

They will land it smart

But not too smartingly.

You see, there's this guy

See there's this guy

And he's really in love

He doesn't know why

But he says what he says

You see there's this girl

And she says to this guy

You gotta move on

But in so many words

It's so hard to hear

But it's easy to say

So she says it to him

And he hears it again

He can't understand

So she has to repeat

But you see there's this guy

And he's really in love.

I love you, ouch

I love you, ouch

I say you in pain

I say you in shock

And I say you surprised

I love you, ouch

I know you're a word

But I say you sometimes

When there's no other word

There is someone I know

They are so much in pain

They are so much rejected

There is no better word

So, I love you, ouch

I hope you'll be there

When I say you in pain

And I say you sometimes.

The night before Halloween

I came from her

Was walking

No, was floating

Cause I came from her

Was floating

No, was flying

No, was soaring

Cause I came away

From her, my mind

Was running

No, was racing

Cause I'd never met

Amazing, like she

Was that night

No words could ever

Really say.

I need my knees

I need my knees

To help me pray

And never mind

My pressing hands

A prayer does come

From lower down

So like a voice

A diaphragm

I do depend

Upon my knees

I need my knees

To lift my prayer

Oh, let me kneel

So in despair

But let me keep

My knees to pray.

The Sand

He wanted beach

To never end

And carried in

His pocket, sand

"Without the sand

It cannot end."

He said, and took

Some sand away

He once did

Love a lady, he

Had wanted love

To never end

He carried in

His pocket, sand

And finely sifted

Grains of her.

A Door

A door is made

To stop the wind

To keep the heat

And fire in

To hold the cold

And wolf at bay

To make the

Salesman turn away

To be a thing

To gently close

To sometimes be

A thing to slam

To open to a

Welcome friend

For keeping out

For letting in.

The age of math

How old am I?

I'm twenty two,

Add nothing, then

Subtract thirteen

Divide by three

Add one, then

Multiply by four

Then add four more

Reduce by three

Add five, then

Multiply by three

Divide by six

Divide again

By one, then

Multiply by four

Subtract by five.

One Day

One day, Minneapolis

Did realize his love

For St. Paul, it had grown

As if ivy on stone

And he'd felt it grow

Tried to trim it away

But he loved their walks

By the river

He had known, he'd seen

He'd felt, he'd known

How the ivy would grow

Till it covered the stone

They had walked by the river

They were quiet, were calm

While their hands intertwined

As if ivy.

Porsche, Check

Porsche, check

I've got the car

You get the car

You get the babes

You get the money

Get the car

You get the babes

You get respect

You get the Porsche

Porsche, check

You get the money

Get the car

You get the babes

You get respect

You get the Porsche

Porsche, check

You get the money

Get the babes.

Jack

Jack went up

To fetch a pail

And Jack leapt

Over candle flame

Jack would only

Eat the lean

And Jack did plant

A magic bean

What is in this

Name of Jack

That lends dynamic

Properties?

But look how Jack

Does leap and play

And sew and fetch

And waste away.

The cat on the stove

I am a cat

Beside a stove

I reach a paw

But pull it back

The stove is hot

But cooling off

I touch it

It is cooler now

I touch again

It's cooler still

And finally

The stove is cool

I am a cat

Upon a stove

Smiling, sitting

Comfortably.

The Coffee's Age

The coffee's age?

Let's say it's ten

Does that make coffee

Old or young?

That many months

Ago the coffee

Made the two

Of us today

The coffee then

Was us begun

Let's count the months

The coffee made

And say it's ten

The coffee's age

How many, many,

Many months?

England

I climb beyond

Its glass and pier

Beyond its meadowland

And sea

Beyond its ancient

History

This country that

Absorbs my eye

With graying stone

And throne and crown

And cliffs and sea

And majesty

I look, and in

My inner eye

I climb beyond

Its castle wall.

The Hummingbird

Oh hummingbird

That sips the sun

What joy you bring

In hovering!

You made the two

Of us as one.

What joy you bring

And can you sing?

You touched us with

Your hovering.

I wonder, can

You sing as well?

Or is it that

You joyful sing

But only with

Your hovering?

June

Of June, I want

The two of us

To think of how

She tossed her hair

Her laughter sailing

Through the air

Those lovely flowers

That she grew!

Of June, I want

Us fondly to

Remember how she

Caught the sun

And held it in

Her open palm

I want not much

But want us to

Remember everything

Of June.

The Bridge

I stand one side

And you, a side

There is a gap

An empty space

There is no bridge

We cannot meet

We smile, we shout

We jump, we wave

We love so much

We fill the space

We smile, we shout

We jump, we wave

In time, we merely

Walk across

And hold each other

Quietly.

It's not about furniture

The sofa? Here

No, over here

The sofa, yeah

The sofa's good

The table? Chairs?

Go over here

The sofa? Yes

The sofa's fine

The sofa? Sure

The sofa's great!

The sofa's wonderful

In fact!

The sofa? No

The sofa's wrong!

It's wrong! All wrong!

Oh, what's the use?!

May you look back in regret

Remember when

Much further on

You have not what

You had, and when

You have no broad

Select of men

But then are old

And overseen

Your summer leaves

That having been

Are no more green

Remember when

Your pretty bird

Was still in song

Remember me

When further on.

No great circumference

Look at me!

Around the world

Around the world

And back again

And here I go

Around again

The man who goes

Around the world!

I'm going now

I'm off again!

I'm off to circle

Round and round

And round and round

And back again

Alas! My world

Is very small.

The thing that's really bothering you

Pull up the floor

And find the floor

The floor that lies

Beneath the floor

Always there is

Something more

Beneath what lies

Beneath the floor

Beneath the thing

That lies beneath

The thing that lies

Beneath the floor

Is something

Under something more

Always the thing

Beneath the floor.

Young and Dumb

Let's be young

Too young to care

Too wise to know

How dumb we are

Too self-absorbed

To see ourselves

Too devil may

To give a damn

Too caught up in

The present, and

Too wild and free

And laissez faire

Too in the moment

Everywhere

Oh, let's be young

Too young to care!

Seething

A fist is made

So mad, a fist

Is made, but just

As soon released

Is made again

And then a face

Becomes a fist

The face in pain

The face in anger

Face in pain, then

Anger, then

In pain again

In twisted, angry

Clenching pain

A fist is made

Then made again.

You tell the man!

My father said

"You tell the man!

You don't just stand

There looking dumb!

You tell the man!

You see something

You want to buy?

You don't just stare!

You tell the man!

Now tell him boy!

He ain't got time!

It ain't no shame!

You figure what

You want, and then

You speak right up!

You tell the man!"

Everyday Things

I want to talk

Of everyday things

Infatuation, ache

And love, and

Passion till

It's maddening

Extreme emotion,

Blood and tears

And desperate,

Longing, pleading looks

And deep embraces,

Poetry, and

Gasping, breathless

Wrenching need

I want to talk

Of everyday things.

Writer's Block

Where's the key?

I've lost the key!

The key! The key!

I've lost the key!

I put it down

I walked away

Oh God! I musn't

Panic so!

I must retrace

My every step

I'll find it yet

I must! The key!

The lock is me

But where's the key?

The key is lost!

Oh God! Oh God!

Potatoes have eyes

Potatoes have eyes

So watch what you say

If potatoes have eyes

Then they probably have ears

If potatoes have ears

Then they probably have tongues

And you know they have skin

So they probably have hair

If potatoes have brains

And they use them to think

Of the so many things

They would do if they could

Then you know that because

We exploit them for food

That they're not thinking

Anything good.

Love can be hard to remember

Here's us,

On vacation.

Here's us traveling,

That was so much fun!

I can't remember

Why, or where

We went, or even

What we did.

Hey look! This

One is you and me,

I can't remember

When that was.

Oh, looking through

These photos always

Makes me feel

A little sad.

The Lonely Stallion

The stallion did

As if the mare

Was there, and all

The things he did

He did as if

The mare was there

And with him in

The grassy field

His gentle, loving

Nuzzles met the air

He couldn't understand

But sadly

Stallion did as

He would do

As if the

Mare was there.

The Intoxicated Man

A raving man

Ran out of the bar

Exclaiming "Now,

I'll drink the air!"

He seemed beyond

Preventing, for

This raving man

His mind was made

His drinking tab

Already paid, and

Running out

Was raving mad

Then in the street

Exclaiming loud

He shouted, "Now, I'll

Drink the air!"

A Lamp Alone

A lamp is light

But light alone

We think, but do

We really see?

A fire's light

In high degree

It's also heat

And shadow play

The lamp alone

Is lacking in

The things we need

To really see

The light, the heat,

The play, the three

Are indispensable

For light.

The Smiling Piano

The player squirms

Uncomfortably

He stands to bow

Resumes his seat

His finished piece

Then so says he

"The damn thing won't

Stop smiling at me!"

He strides away

The notes all fade

Piano so well

Played, but still,

He stomps away

And so says he

"That damn thing won't

Stop smiling at me!"

About the author

Terence Mark Winstead lives in Minnesota. He enjoys reading, writing, running, travel, and imagining. He is the author of novels, poetry, plays, and short stories.

Made in the USA
Monee, IL
07 June 2022